CIPS STUDY M

ADVANCED DIPLOMA IN PROCUREMENT AND SUPPLY

REVISION NOTES

Improving the competitiveness of supply chains

Printed and distributed by:

The Chartered Institute of Procurement & Supply, Easton House, Easton on the Hill, Stamford, Lincolnshire PE9 3NZ
Tel: +44 (0) 1780 756 777
Fax: +44 (0) 1780 751 610
Email: info@cips.org
Website: www.cips.org

First edition October 2012
Reprinted with minor amendments June 2016

Contents

Preface

Welcome to your Revision Notes.

Your Revision Notes are a summarised version of the material contained in your Course Book. If you find that the Revision Notes refer to material that you do not recollect clearly, you should refer back to the Course Book to refresh your memory.

There is space at the end of each chapter in your Revision Notes where you can enter your own notes for reference.

A note on style

Throughout your Study Packs you will find that we use the masculine form of personal pronouns. This convention is adopted purely for the sake of stylistic convenience – we just don't like saying 'he/she' all the time. Please don't think this reflects any kind of bias or prejudice.

June 2016

CHAPTER 1

Supply Chains and Supply Chain Management

Supply chains and networks

The role of procurement has developed over recent decades, to reflect the increasing integration of management activities. Changing focus of procurement:

- **Clerical (transactional):** purchasing is perceived as a low-ranking routine function, characterised by a focus on internal performance and efficiency.
- **Commercial:** the focus shifts to price and cost savings, obtained mainly through the interface with suppliers.
- **Strategic (proactive):** the focus is on procurement making an effective contribution to competitive advantage.

The concept of 'supply chain management' sees all the 'players' in the flow of value towards the customer as an integrated value-adding and competitive system.

In relation to the 'focal firm' suppliers are said to be upstream and customers are said to be downstream.

The management of a firm's immediate upstream and downstream relationships is still important. However, these kinds of focused buyer-supplier exchanges usually happen within the context of a lengthier supply process. An **inter-business supply chain** is a linked sequence of contributors in different firms.

The chain metaphor highlights several useful characteristics:

- It emphasises 'serial co-operation'.
- It emphasises mutual dependency and collaboration.
- It emphasises the importance of 'linkages' between members.
- It is continuous and non-directional.

The supply chain concept can be applied *within* organisations – as well as *between* them. The internal supply chain (or value chain) describes a similar flow of information and other resources *within* – into and through – a given organisation: from inbound activities (procuring and receiving inputs), to conversion activities (transforming inputs into outputs) to outbound activities (moving outputs onward to customers). This is an important idea for the **internal customer concept**.

Even a tiered supply chain model offers a simplified picture. In reality, each organisation in the supply chain has multiple other relationships with its own customers, suppliers, industry contacts, partners and advisers – a supply network.

- This is a more strategic model for supply chain relationships.
- It raises the possibility of a wider range of collaborations.
- It recognises the potential of 'extended enterprises'.
- It recognises that extended enterprises may overlap.

Value adding strategies from supply chain thinking:

- Value engineering
- Lean supply
- Agile supply
- Value-adding negotiations and relationships

Supply chain management (SCM)

CIPS defines supplier management as: 'Managing the supplier in order to extract additional value and benefits as a result of the relationship'.

The term 'supply chain management' is often used both:

- In a specific and technical sense, to refer to a particular, modern strategic approach to supply network relationships and management
- In a more loose and general sense, to refer to the role of a procurement function in managing not just transactions, but suppliers and end-to-end supply chain activity.

The shift to supply chain management

TRADITIONAL WAYS	NEW WAYS
Key feature: Independence	Key feature: Integration
Independent of next link	Dependency
Links are protective	End-to-end visibility
Uncertainty	More certainty
Unresponsive to change	Quicker response
High cost, low service	High service, lower cost
Fragmented internally	'Joined up' structures
'Blame' (adversarial) culture	'Gain' (collaborative value-adding) culture
Competing companies	Competing supply chains

Key features of supply chain management:

- Building co-operative relationships
- Building effective business processes
- Integrating across functional and organisational boundaries

Structuring supply chains and networks

Slack, Chambers and Johnston (*Operations Management)* highlight an overall supply network perspective as significant, because it highlights three important design decisions.

- How should the network be configured?
- Where should each part of the network owned by the organisation be located?
- What physical capability should each part of the network owned by the company have?

There is a trade-off between the desire to minimise the costs and complexity of managing a large supplier network and the desire to minimise the risks of having a very narrow supplier base (creating vulnerability through dependency on a small number of suppliers). One of the solutions to this trade-off lies in the way the supply chain is structured: specifically, in the development of **supplier tiering**.

The implications of supply chain tiering:

- The sourcing, selection and contracting of the first-tier suppliers will be a crucial strategic exercise.
- There will be fewer commercial relationships to manage.
- The top-tier organisation will still need to 'drill down' through the tiers in the supply chain.
- The buyer may exercise influence over the first-tier supplier to adopt some of its own existing suppliers as subcontractors or lower-tier suppliers.
- More and better supply chain improvements and innovations may be available.
- Procurement may be freed up to pursue a more strategic focus.

The responsibility for disposal and recycling of end products has shifted to producers and importers. These developments have given rise to the closed loop supply chain and an increased emphasis on reverse logistics.

The term 'network sourcing' is properly used in a technical sense to refer to a particular pattern of buyer-supplier interaction that has developed as a result of certain elements in the Japanese-style subcontracting system. The concept was originated by Professor Itsutomo Mitsui and introduced to mainstream supply chain management thinking by Peter Hines.

One of the ways positive supplier relationships can be leveraged for supply chain improvement and competitiveness is by 'broadening supply'. The organisation can manage supply risk by having *more* potential suppliers of a given item or category of purchases, pre-qualified and approved as being able to meet its requirements.

More commonly, however, strong collaborative supplier relationships are used to 'narrow supply', enabling purchases to be concentrated on a smaller group of developed and trusted supply partners. *Supplier base rationalisation* (or optimisation) is concerned with determining roughly how many suppliers the buying firm wants to do business with. This enables the firm to:

- Control procurement costs
- Leverage the potential of closer, long-term, collaborative relationships
- Avoid waste
- Maintain the security of supply.

Risks of this approach:

- Over-dependence on a few suppliers
- Supply disruption
- The loss of preferred suppliers' goodwill and co-operation
- Preferred suppliers growing complacent
- Being 'locked in' to unsuitable suppliers
- Missing out on seeking or utilising new or more competitive suppliers

The concept of **repositioning** an organisation within the supply or value chain implies the extension of its operations or control to a wider range of upstream or downstream activities – and a greater share of responsibility for creating and adding value.

Repositioning strategies include: organic or internal development and diversification into activities one step up or down the chain; acquisition of, or merger with, organisations one step up or down the chain; and/or strategic collaboration and integration with organisations one step up or down the chain. These are essentially growth strategies. Repositioning may also, however, include withdrawal or contraction: outsourcing or subcontracting activities, say, or divesting from activities, in order to narrow the organisation's focus to its core competencies.

Value-adding supply chains

Value is the 'worth' of the product or service, which may be measured in two ways: what it costs the organisation to produce or provide, and what customers are willing to pay for it. In other words:

- An organisation creates value – by performing its activities more effectively or efficiently than its competitors *and*
- Customers purchase value – by comparing an organisation's products and services with those of its competitors.

'Drivers' for SCM:

- Cost pressures
- Time pressures
- Reliability pressures
- Response pressures
- Transparency pressures
- Globalisation pressure

Benefits of an SCM approach:

- 'Supply chains compete, not companies.'
- Reduced total costs
- Improved responsiveness to customer requirements
- Access to complementary resources and capabilities
- Enhanced product and service quality
- Improved supply chain communication
- Improved inventory management
- Reduced cycle times
- Greater transparency for cost and risk management
- Greater supply chain visibility
- Optimising the balance of service levels and costs

Adding value through the supply chain:

- Selecting suppliers with quality management systems (eg ISO 9000)
- Appraising the quality management systems and 'track record' of suppliers
- Preparing preferred or approved supplier lists
- Influencing the quality of product design by early supplier involvement
- Translating design requirements into specifications
- Developing goods inwards procedures for quality inspection and testing
- Managing relationships with suppliers
- Monitoring and controlling suppliers' quality performance
- Working with suppliers to resolve quality disputes
- Reduced prices and total costs
- Reducing time to market
- Creating innovation
- Reducing risk and supply chain vulnerability

Own notes

CHAPTER 2

Infrastructure and Processes

Theoretical perspectives on added value

An organisation can add value by inducing customers to pay more, and/or by reducing costs or increasing the efficiency of processes.

Organisations can thus add value through enhancing product quality or design; value for money; delivery or availability; brand appeal; exclusivity; service levels; and so on. Porter and others have emphasised that value is effectively 'in the eye of the customer'.

The **value chain** is the sequence of business activities by which value is added to the products or services produced by an organisation or supply chain. It embraces the entire process from raw materials to finished delivered product and continuing after-sales service. Porter's value chain model defines primary activities (inbound logistics, operations, outbound logistics, marketing and sales, and service) and support activities (firm infrastructure, HRM, technology development, and procurement).

The individual firm's value chain does not exist in isolation, and value-adding activities do not stop at the organisation's boundaries. Competitive advantage can be achieved anywhere along the internal business value chain – but a firm must also secure competitive advantage by managing the *linkages within its supply network:* the basis of techniques such as lean and agile supply, total quality management and supply chain management.

A key point of the value chain and value network models, for the purpose of contract and supplier relationship management, is that activities within the value system are recognised as *interdependent:* each element can affect the costs, efficiency or effectiveness of another in the value chain, forming what Porter called 'linkages'. Linkages are the interactions between different value chains along a supply chain, which ultimately meet the demands of the final consumer.

Porter argued that the development of linkages can often lead to competitive advantage via (a) optimisation and (b) co-ordination.

Activities and processes which add cost, without adding value, are identified as 'waste' activities. They contribute nothing to the flow of value to the customer – and should therefore be minimised or eliminated throughout the supply chain where possible. Waste minimisation is a priority process for supply chain improvement.

'Each activity within a value chain provides inputs which, after processing, constitute *added value to the output received by the ultimate customer* in the form of a product or service'. Procurement can therefore be seen as an integral part of the flow of value *to the end customer* – not just as an internal administrative support function.

Problems with Porter's value chain model:

- It defines value creation as the profit margin of each firm – rather than a whole-chain focus on consumer satisfaction.
- The model is not highly integrative.
- The distinction between primary and support functions is arbitrary.
- It is a static model, based solely on American firms.

Aspects of organisational infrastructure

Organisational infrastructure *underpins* business processes: providing the organisational context and structures for the flow of work and information required. Elements of organisational infrastructure may either *support or undermine* processes.

Purposes of formal organisation structure:

- To define work roles and relationships
- To define work tasks and responsibilities
- To channel information flows efficiently through the organisation
- To coordinate goals and activities of different units
- To control the flow of work, information and resources
- To support flexible working and adaptability
- To encourage and support the commitment, involvement and satisfaction of the people who work for the organisation
- To support and improve the efficiency, effectiveness and competitiveness of the organisation's performance through all of the above

Modern approaches to organisation and management have emphasised that most organisations exist in a changing environment and must adapt in order to survive. Organisation structures should be adapted to the stability or dynamism of their market environments.

Modern trends in flexible organisation:

- The flattening of organisation hierarchies
- Chunked structures
- Project management
- Horizontal structures
- Core-periphery structures
- Network structures
- Virtual structures

One of the key issues in structural efficiency (and managerial control) is the extent to which structures are **centralised or decentralised**. Each offers advantages for a procurement function. Responsibilities for supply management activities at a higher level (policy development, purchasing research, supply chain development, major contract negotiations and so on) should be centralised.

Hybrid models and approaches to support **co-ordinated decentralisation**:

- The **CLAN** (centre-led action network) approach
- The **SCAN** (strategically-controlled action network) approach
- The **lead buyer** approach
- A **business partnering** approach

Tools for changing organisational culture:

- Consistent expression and modelling of the new values by management
- Changing underlying assumptions, values and beliefs
- Use of HRM mechanisms or supplier management mechanisms

Supply chain improvement may require the **development** and/or **introduction** of systems which are currently lacking. Supply chain competitiveness and performance may also require the improvement of existing technology and systems.

Process mapping and management

Analysing a business operation or process enables identification of:

- Sources of process inefficiency and non-value-adding activity
- Sources of process ineffectiveness
- Points of process complexity
- Points of risk
- Points of cost, where there is scope for cost reduction
- Points of profit and opportunity

Such analysis can be assisted by the use of diagrammatic techniques, such as flowcharts or IDEF mapping.

Value stream mapping is used to identify, demonstrate and decrease waste in supply and manufacturing processes.

Supply chain mapping is a tool enabling managers to identify:

- Strong and weak linkages in the value chain
- Potential areas of supply risk
- Potential areas of sustainability, compliance or reputational risk
- Potential areas of opportunity or strength
- Areas of inefficiency in the supply chain
- Potential efficiencies
- The breakdown of costs, added value and profit at each stage of the supply chain

- Areas in which improved information or resource flows are required
- Weakness in reverse logistics
- Areas in which the organisation may need to move from a 'chain' to a 'network'.

Value chain analysis utilises Porter's value chain model to identify potential for the elimination of wastes and the addition of further value at various points and activities in the value chain. In its most basic form, the process of value chain analysis thus involves:

- Identifying sub-activities for each primary activity and support activity
- Identifying linkages
- Looking for opportunities to increase value

A less structured, simplified approach to value chain analysis, such as you might use in an exam case study, comprises a three-step process.

- Activity analysis
- Value analysis
- Evaluation and planning

Managing the sourcing process

The sourcing process is an essentially linear model of what may take place in the course of a typical procurement exercise, from identification of need to performance (satisfaction of the need): you might depict it as a linear flowchart. However, it is also possible to view procurement activity as a 'cycle' or continuous loop, because further needs will constantly emerge, requiring ongoing repetition of the procurement process.

Managing stages in the sourcing process:

- Identifying business needs – eg by challenging user definitions of business needs
- Specification – eg challenging specifications, or involving cross-functional teams
- Surveying and engaging the market – eg use of purchasing research
- Sourcing plan – eg by evaluation of alternative sourcing options
- Supplier pre-qualification and appraisal – eg by ensuring robust appraisal procedures
- Supplier selection and contract award – eg by use of competition
- Contract development and communication – eg by use of formal written contracts
- Contract management – eg by efficient management of purchase to pay processes
- Supplier performance management – eg by effective risk management
- Relationship management – eg by regular contact, communication and information sharing

The purpose of supplier appraisal, evaluation or pre-qualification is to ensure that a potential supplier will be able to perform any contract that it is awarded, to the required standard. For the exam, it is useful to memorise Carter's 10Cs of supplier appraisal.

Value-adding benefits of proactive post-contract management of supplier relationships and performance:

- The company incurs lower costs of identifying, appraising and training new vendors.

- Quality and other problems can be ironed out progressively.
- Goodwill developed with positive relationships may earn preferential treatment or flexibility from suppliers in the event of emergencies.
- Suppliers may be more motivated to give their best performance.
- Motivated suppliers may be willing to co-invest.
- There is less risk of supplier failure or poor performance.

Optimising sourcing decisions:

- In-house or outsource
- Supplier selection
- Procurement
- Sourcing-related metrics

Own notes

CHAPTER 3

Approaches to Supply Chain Improvement

The relationship spectrum

Relationship spectrum: adversarial; arm's length; transactional; closer tactical; single sourced; outsourcing; strategic alliance; partnership; co-destiny.

Cox's **stepladder of contractual relationships**

- Adversarial leverage
- Preferred suppliers
- Single sourcing
- Network sourcing and partnerships
- Strategic supplier alliances or joint ventures

There is a modern trend away from adversarial relationships and towards closer collaboration with suppliers, at least for supplies that are strategic and critical. The buyer seeks to develop long-term, mutually-beneficial relationships with a smaller number of preferred suppliers.

The most appropriate relationship type for a given purchasing situation may depend on factors such as the following.

- The nature and importance of the items being purchased
- The competence, capability, co-operation and performance of the supplier
- Geographical distance
- The compatibility of the supply partners
- The organisation's and purchasing function's objectives and priorities
- Supply market conditions
- Legal and regulatory requirements

The collaborative model of supply chain management

With a *transactional* approach, the benefits of doing business together arise purely from exchange: money in return for goods or services. In a *relational* approach, the benefits of doing business together arise from sharing, collaboration and synergy (2 + 2 = 5).

Features of a constructive supply partnership:

- Joint and mutual search for greater efficiency and competitiveness
- Joint planning for the future by the customer and the supplier
- Agreed shared objectives
- Joint effort to eliminate waste from the supply chain
- Openness and transparency between the organisations
- Understanding the expectations of the other party
- Relationship of equal partners
- Prepared and agreed exit strategy

Drivers of collaborative supply chain relationships:

- Whole supply chains – not just individual firms – compete with each other.
- There is a need for faster product development.
- Organisations are increasingly outsourcing non-core activities.
- ICT developments have enabled and supported inter-organisational networking.
- There is pressure for companies to protect and leverage their intellectual property.
- Arms' length, opportunistic transactions fail to leverage the competitive and value-adding potential in supply chain relationships.
- There are costs of adversarial relationships.
- Closer relationships and integration help to reduce waste in supply chains.
- 'Best practice' supply techniques, such as total quality management and just in time supply, reduce tolerance for delays and errors in the supply process.
- There has been a major shift towards relationship marketing.

Key characteristics of partnership sourcing:

- Cultural compatibility between the partners
- A high level of trust, knowledge sharing and openness
- Mutual acceptance of 'win-win' within the supply chain
- Relevant expertise, resources or competencies in complementary areas
- Clear joint objectives and meaningful performance measures
- The use of cross-functional teams
- A total quality management philosophy
- A high degree of systems integration

Advantages and disadvantages of partnering

ADVANTAGES FOR THE BUYER	DISADVANTAGES FOR THE BUYER
Greater stability of supply and supply prices	Risk of complacency re cost and quality
Sharing of risk and investment	Less flexibility to change suppliers at need
Better supplier motivation and responsiveness, arising from mutual commitment and reciprocity	Possible risk to confidentiality, intellectual property (eg if suppliers also supply competitors)
Cost savings from reduced supplier base, collaborative cost reduction	May be locked into relationship with an incompatible or inflexible supplier
Access to supplier's technology and expertise	May be restricted – eg in EU public sector procurement directives (eg re-tendering after 3–5 years)
Joint planning and information sharing, supporting capacity planning and efficiency	May be locked into relationship, despite supply market changes and opportunities
Ability to plan long-term improvements	Costs of relationship management
More attention to relationship management: eg access to an account manager	Mutual dependency may create loss of flexibility and control
ADVANTAGES FOR THE SUPPLIER	DISADVANTAGES FOR THE SUPPLIER
Greater stability and volume of business, enabling investment in development	May be locked into relationship with an incompatible or inflexible customer
Working with customers, enabling improved service, learning and development	Gains and risks may not be fairly shared in the partnership (depending on power balance)
Joint planning and information sharing, supporting capacity planning and efficiency	Risk of customer exploiting transparency (eg on costings, to force prices down)
Sharing of risk and investment	Investment in relationship management
Cost savings from efficiency, collaborative cost reduction, payment on time	Dependency on customer may create loss of flexibility and control
Access to customer's technology and expertise	May be restricted – eg by EU public sector procurement directives
More attention to relationship management: eg access to a vendor manager	May be locked into relationship, despite market changes and opportunities

The competitive model of supply chain management

In adversarial or competitive relationships, each party seeks to obtain the best possible outcome for itself, at the expense of the other party if necessary. Such relationships are characterised by: lack of trust; transaction focus; use of power and negotiation; enforced compliance with contract terms; little recognition of mutual interests.

Arguments in support of the competitive supply model:

- A more competitive approach may secure the best commercial deal.

- A competitive approach may help to maintain competitiveness of supply.
- It may be required to avoid supplier complacency.
- Developing collaborative relationships takes time and effort, and it is unrealistic to devote such resources to *all* relationships.
- There are risks in long-term relationships.

Reasons for changing or switching suppliers:

- Problems with the performance or reliability of the existing supplier
- A new supplier offering a more competitive bid
- A new supplier being better able to capitalise on emerging opportunities
- Low-risk, widely available, standardised items being sourced through arms' length, transactional purchasing approaches

If switching does take place, here are some key issues for buyers.

- The need for early flagging of contracts up for renewal
- The need for proactive transition planning and risk management

An organisation may need to develop a *portfolio* of relationships.

- Using the Pareto principle or 80: 20 rule
- Using a blend of approaches (eg an 'adversarial-collaborative' approach)

Outsourcing

Make/do or buy decisions at three levels of planning: strategic; tactical; operational. Factors involved in the decision:

- Whether the item or activity is strategically important or 'core' to the business
- Economic factors
- The availability of in-house competencies and production capacity
- The availability of suitable external suppliers
- The assessed risks of devolving activities to the external supply chain

Drivers for outsourcing:

- Quality drivers
- Cost drivers
- Business focus drivers
- Financial drivers
- Relationship drivers
- Human resource drivers

Advantages and disadvantages of outsourcing

ADVANTAGES/BENEFITS	DISADVANTAGES/RISKS
Supports organisational rationalisation and downsizing	Potentially higher cost of services (including contractor profit margin)
Allows focused investment of managerial, staff and other resources on the organisation's core activities and competencies	Difficulty of ensuring service quality and consistency and corporate social responsibility
Accesses and leverages the specialist expertise, technology and resources of contractors	Potential loss of in-house expertise, knowledge, contacts or technologies
Access to economies of scale since contractors may serve many customers	Potential loss of control over key areas of performance and risk
Adds competitive performance incentives	Added distance from the customer or end-user, by having an intermediary service provider
Leverages collaborative supply relationships, and can support synergies	Risks of 'lock in' to an incompatible or under-performing relationship
Cost certainty (negotiated contract price) for activities where demand and costs are uncertain or fluctuating: shared financial risks	Risks of loss of control over confidential data and intellectual property

Core competencies are distinctive value-creating skills, capabilities and resources which:

- Add value in the eyes of the customer
- Are scarce and difficult for competitors to imitate
- Are flexible for future needs
- Offer sustainable competitive advantage

Competencies and contractor competence

Core importance / *Competence of contractors*	High	Low
Low	**Outsource/buy in**	**Develop contracting**
High	**Collaboration**	**In-house**

Reasons why outsourcing fails:

- The organisation fails to distinguish correctly between core and non-core activities.
- The organisation fails to identify and select a suitable supplier.
- The organisation has unrealistic expectations of the outsource provider.
- The outsourcing contract contains inadequate or inappropriate terms and conditions.
- The contract does not contain well defined key performance indicators.
- The organisation lacks management skills to control performance.
- The organisation gradually surrenders control of performance to the contractor.

Globalised production and procurement

Globalisation is 'the increasing integration of internationally dispersed economic activity': globalisation of markets, of supply, and of production.

The term 'offshoring' refers to the relocation of business processes to a lower cost location, usually overseas. This practice is in essence a form of outsourcing, but the overseas element gives rise to additional considerations. Apart from the possible cost savings, supporters of offshoring point to the benefits of free trade, providing jobs to the poorer country.

Opportunities available from international sourcing:

- Access to supplies which may not be available in local markets
- Access to a wider supplier base
- Opportunities for cost savings
- Competitive quality
- Reduced regulatory and compliance burden
- Leveraging available ICT developments for virtual organisation, e-sourcing and e-procurement, contract management and supplier relationship management and communication
- Ability to compete with competitors who are benefiting from any or all of the above advantages

The downside of international sourcing:

- Socio-cultural differences
- Language barriers
- Legal issues
- Logistical and supply risks
- Technical risk
- Increased security risks to personnel and operations
- Exchange rate risk
- Payment risk
- Difficulties of monitoring and assuring quality, environmental and ethical standards
- General STEEPLE factor risks in the overseas environment

The key principle of low cost country sourcing is to obtain sourcing efficiencies by identifying and exploiting cost differentials between countries or geographical regions. However, some low-cost, developing countries pose significant business, supply and sustainability risks to buying organisations, and may *not* be an appropriate target for low-cost country sourcing.

There will need to be a strong emphasis on:

- Identification and prioritisation of opportunities to lower costs and improve supply chain competitiveness
- Risk assessment and 'due diligence' on potential suppliers
- Bridging cultural gaps in dealing with developing economy suppliers
- Investment in supplier development
- Ongoing productivity improvements

Own notes

Own notes

CHAPTER 4

Total Quality Management

Defining quality

Garvin's five approaches to quality:

- The transcendent approach
- The user-based approach
- The product-based approach
- The manufacturing-based approach
- The value-based approach

Garvin's eight dimensions of quality:

- Performance
- Features
- Reliability
- Durability
- Conformance
- Serviceability
- Aesthetics
- Perceived quality

Most important definitions of 'right quality' for a buyer:

- *Fitness for purpose or use*
- *Conformance to requirement or specification*
- *Comparative excellence*

The management and control of quality is an aspect of risk management.

Quality-related costs include *both*:

- The cost of appraisal and prevention activities, designed to minimise poor quality products entering the production process and/or reaching the customer – *and*
- The cost of 'failure': losses incurred because of poor quality products entering the production process and/or reaching the customer.

The costs of ensuring and assuring quality include prevention costs and appraisal costs.

Internal failure costs are those that arise from quality failure, where the problem is identified and corrected *before* the finished product or service reaches the customer. **External failure costs** are those that arise from quality failure identified and corrected *after* the finished product or service reaches the customer.

Approaches to quality

Quality control is based on the concept of **defect detection**. Inspection forms an integral part of most quality control systems, and is usually based on a process of 'sampling', whereby a small number of items is considered as statistically representative of a whole 'population' of items.

Limitations of quality control:

- A very large number of items has to be inspected to prevent defective items from reaching customers.
- Defect tolerances may be unacceptably high.
- The process identifies mistakes which have already incurred costs.
- Inspection tends to be duplicated at each stage of the process.

Quality assurance is a more integrated and proactive approach, based on **defect prevention**. It seeks to build quality into every stage of the process from concept and specification onwards.

A **quality management system (QMS)** is: 'A set of co-ordinated activities to direct and control an organisation in order to continually improve the effectiveness and efficiency of its performance'. The main purpose of a QMS is to define and manage processes for systematic quality assurance.

ISO 9000 comprises a family of quality management standards, built around business processes, with an emphasis on improvement and on meeting the needs of customers.

The term 'total quality management' is generally used to refer to a radical approach to quality management, as a total business paradigm or philosophy. TQM is an orientation to quality in which quality values and aspirations are applied to the management of all resources and relationships within the firm – and throughout the supply chain – in order to seek continuous improvement and excellence in all aspects of performance.

Supply chain relationships are important in quality management.

In a quality management environment the recognition of, and service to, the internal customer is critical.

- Internal operational interfaces must be professionally developed and efficient.
- Organisation structures based on functional specialisms and 'silos' are increasingly being replaced by 'horizontalised' cross-functional structures, as organisations re-engineer to become more process-focused, flexible and responsive.

Managing service quality

A service is 'any activity or benefit that one party can offer to another that is essentially intangible and does not result in ownership of anything'. When it comes to specifying and managing quality, services present problems additional to those that arise in purchasing materials or manufactured goods.

- Services are *intangible*.
- Services are *variable*.
- It is hard to assess the many factors involved in providing a quality service.

General quality dimensions for services have been developed as part of an assessment tool called *SERVQUAL*.

- Tangibles
- Reliability
- Responsiveness
- Assurance
- Empathy

Service quality definition may be set out by the customer in the service specification, contract key performance indicators, or a **service level agreement** (SLA): a formal statement of performance requirements, specifying the nature and level of service to be provided by a service supplier.

A wide range of techniques is available for monitoring service provision and service levels, and feeding back the data in order to identify 'service gaps' which need to be addressed.

- Observation and experience
- Spot checks and sample testing
- Business results and indirect indicators
- Customer and user feedback
- Electronic performance monitoring
- Self-assessment by the service provider
- Collaborative performance review

Total quality management

Mullins synthesises various definitions of TQM as expressing: 'a way of life for an organisation as a whole, committed to total customer satisfaction through a continuous process of improvement, and the contribution and involvement of people'.

Principles of TQM:

- Customers are the ultimate definers of value, and the ultimate drivers for delivering quality
- Quality management requires the design and management of processes to meet customer needs cost-effectively and competitively
- Quality management requires everyone in the organisation (and, increasingly, across the supply chain) to view everything in terms of meeting customer needs – and to be involved in meeting customer needs.

Values of a TQM approach:

- Focus on the customer
- Quality chains
- Quality culture
- Total involvement
- Quality through people
- Team-based management
- Get it right first time
- Process alignment
- Quality management systems
- Continuous improvement or *kaizen*
- Sharing best practice

Limitations of TQM:

- TQM can prove limited in practice.
- TQM can be disruptive.
- TQM is time-consuming, costly and difficult to introduce.

Perspectives on total quality

The philosophy of TQM has evolved over decades of practical experience, and through the research and advocacy of certain influential authorities on the subject (sometimes referred to as 'the quality gurus').

W Edwards Deming formulated a list of the 'seven deadly diseases of management'.

- Lack of constancy of purpose
- Emphasis on short-term profits
- Evaluation of individual performance, by merit rating, or annual review
- Mobility of management, or managerial job turnover
- Running a company on visible figures alone
- Excessive medical costs
- Excessive costs of warranty and legal damage awards

Deming's **fourteen points of management** therefore emphasised measures to support total quality.

Philip Crosby argued that 'quality is free', in the sense that an effective quality system can save an organisation more than it costs to implement, both by reducing failure costs and by increasing revenue through customer satisfaction. He laid down four absolutes or prescriptions for quality.

- Quality is defined as 'conformance to requirements'.
- The system of quality is prevention.
- The performance standard is zero defects: 'getting it right first time'.
- The measurement of quality is the price of non-conformance.

His **14-step plan** offers an action plan for implementing quality improvement.

Joseph Juran defined quality as 'fitness for use', categorising twelve dimensions of quality under four main headings.

- Quality of design
- Quality of conformance
- Quality of availability
- Field service

His later **quality planning map** provides a staged process for understanding quality.

- Identify customers, both internal and external.
- Determine the needs of those customers.
- Translate customer needs into our language.
- Develop a product designed to meet those needs.
- Optimise product features so as to meet both our needs and customers' needs.
- Develop a process that is able to produce the product.
- Optimise the process.
- Prove that the process is effective under operating conditions.
- Transfer the process to operations.

Own notes

CHAPTER 5

Using Performance Data

Performance measurement

Supplier performance measurement is the comparison of a supplier's current performance against: defined performance criteria; previous performance; or the performance of other organisations. It is used for the following purposes.

- Helping to identify the highest-quality and best-performing suppliers
- Suggesting how relationships with suppliers can be enhanced
- Helping to ensure that suppliers live up to what was promised in their contracts
- Providing suppliers with an incentive to maintain and/or continuously improve performance levels
- Significantly improving supplier performance

Performance measures should be SMART: specific; measurable; attainable; relevant; time-bounded.

Benefits of using KPIs:

- Increased and improved communication on performance issues.
- Motivation to achieve or better the specified performance level
- Support for collaborative buyer-supplier relations
- The ability directly to compare year on year performance
- Focus on key results areas
- Clearly defined shared goals
- Reduced conflict

Stages in developing KPIs: identify critical success factors; determine measures of success or improvement for each CSF; agree appropriate KPIs.

Performance measurement at different levels

STRATEGIC	TACTICAL	OPERATIONAL
Lead time against norm	Efficiency of order cycle	Delivery performance (OTIF)
Quality status and aspirations	Quality assurance methodology	Quality conformance or non-conformance rates
Future growth, innovation, and/ or integration potential	Capacity flexibility	Technical support levels
Cost saving initiatives and potential	Cashflow management	Speed of response to change in planned requirements
Risk management processes		

Performance **monitoring** and **review** may be carried out in various ways.

- Continuous monitoring
- Monitoring at key stages
- Periodic reviews
- Post-completion reviews

Feedback mechanisms for supplier performance:

- Gathering of feedback from internal and external customers
- Gathering of performance information through observation, testing and analysis of documentation
- Budgetary control
- Formal performance reviews or appraisals
- Continually monitoring compliance with contract terms
- Regular meetings between buyer and supplier representatives
- Project management
- The use of consultants to monitor compliance with quality standards, benchmarks or ethical standards
- The use of technical specialists to monitor supplier performance

Systematic post-contract performance appraisal and evaluation is often referred to as 'vendor rating'. Vendor rating is the measurement of supplier performance using agreed criteria or KPIs.

One common approach to vendor rating is based on the use of a supplier **performance evaluation form**. Another approach is the **factor rating method,** or **weighted factor scorecard** system.

Introduction to statistics

Methods of probability sampling:

- Simple random sampling
- Systematic sampling
- Stratified sampling
- Cluster sampling
- Multistage sampling

The **arithmetic mean** is the best known type of average. It is defined as the total *value* of the items divided by the total *number* of the items in a data set.

The **median** is calculated as the *middle term* in a data set, once all the items have been arranged in order of magnitude.

The **mode** is the value that *occurs most frequently* among all the items in the data set.

The **range** is the simplest measure of dispersion, being the difference between the extreme values of the distribution: that is highest value *minus* lowest value.

The **standard deviation** is the most valuable and widely used measure of dispersion. However, it is also the most complex to calculate.

There are three main, highly practical statistical distributions (see table).

Probability distributions

	FOCUS	APPLICATIONS
Binomial distribution	The occurrence of discrete events with only two either/or outcomes (eg accept/compliant or reject/non-compliant; possessing or not possessing a specified attribute). Outcomes are expressed as p and q. Probabilities: q + p = 1. So if p = 0.9 , q = 0.1	• Probability of a batch containing defects or non-defects; *x* or more/fewer-than-*x* defects • Customers buying or not buying a brand. • Success or failure of a project; delivery on time or late.
Poisson distribution	The occurrence of discrete events (eg defects) occurring within a continuous medium (eg a process or period of time).	Quality control and risk assessment eg: • Defects in a pipeline (or other continuous medium). • Supplier failures over a time period
Normal distribution	Ranges of possibilities and how likely they are to occur, based on: • Continuous historical data • Formed into a frequency distribution • Diagrammed as a histogram • Showing a distribution curve.	Statistical process control 'If defects are normally distributed, calculate the probability that defects are between 3 and 7 (tolerance level) per delivery'.

If a process has a normal distribution, 99.7% of the data is captured by the curve at three standard deviations from the mean (plus or minus). In other words, there is only a 0.3% probability of finding a value *beyond* +/– 3 standard deviations. Therefore a measurement value outside this central band indicates that the process has shifted, or become unstable or out of control: creating more variability.

Statistical process control (SPC)

The aim of many process improvement techniques is to **reduce variation in the process**; for example, to ensure that all outputs from the process are as nearly as possible identical. One common technique is the use of **control charts.** Control charts are used to plot upper and lower control limits, which define the boundaries of acceptable output. Anything outside this tolerance will be rejected.

SPC is a technique for identifying the possibility of quality defects at an early stage of production. It is designed:

- to impose **control**
- over **processes**
- using **statistical methods**.

The principles are relatively simple. Quality assurance and/or maintenance specialists determine that the process is working the way it should be. The operator begins production and takes samples of output for inspection at short time intervals. The measurements are recorded and, by using statistical analysis, it is established what average measurement is expected for all units of output. A determination of the expected range of measurement is provided. If the measurements taken from samples cluster around this predetermined measurement or average within expected parameters, then the process is in control. If the results are outside the expected parameters then they are not.

This is the strength of the SPC concept, because at this stage the operator can halt production to seek and rectify the fault. Few defective units will have been produced. Once the fault is remedied, production begins again.

One of the limitations of SPC is that it focuses on ensuring that a production process remains in control: that is, operating within its normal level of precision. However, there will be many scenarios in which the 'normal level of precision' will itself be insufficient to meet the buyer's requirements – and in this case, SPC is of no help.

Process capability is a measure of the level of uniformity (absence of variability) that can be achieved by a process under normal operating conditions. If the process capability of a supplier's processes is known, the buyer can compare it with the tolerances (range of variance) he is prepared to accept. If the supplier's process capability falls within the buyer's tolerances, then – provided that the system stays within control while the production run is in progress (which can be managed using SPC) – the buyer can be satisfied that quality requirements will be met.

Failure mode and effects analysis (FMEA) is a technique for determining the different ways (modes) in which a product can fail, and assessing the seriousness of the effects in each case. (The term FMECA, or 'failure mode, effects and criticality analysis', is sometimes used.) By using appropriate numerical parameters, the different modes can be ranked in order of how critical they are – and attention can then be concentrated on the most critical areas.

To conduct the analysis, the following steps are required.

- Identify the components forming part of the product.
- For each component, list the different ways in which failure may occur and the causes of each.
- For each failure mode identified, list the effects on the overall product.
- Assess the probability (**P**) of each failure on a scale of 1 (not very probable) to 10 (extremely probable).
- Assess the seriousness (**S**) of each failure mode by considering its effects, again on a scale of 1 (not very serious) to 10 (extremely serious).
- Assess the difficulty (**D**) of detecting the failure before the customer uses the product, on a scale of 1 (easy to detect) to 10 (very difficult to detect).
- Calculate the criticality index (**C**) for each failure mode by use of the formula:

$C = P \times S \times D$

A low figure for C indicates that the failure mode is less important, ie it may have a low probability of occurrence, or a low seriousness level, or may be of such a nature that discovery is likely before the customer uses the product, or all three of these. If C has a high value it would indicate that urgent attention is required.

Techniques for **diagnosing the causes of process failures** and quality defects: cause and effect analysis, cause-effect-cause analysis, and why-why analysis.

The Six Sigma methodology

Six Sigma is a disciplined application of statistical problem-solving tools to identify and quantify waste and indicate steps for improvement, focusing on three main areas: improving customer satisfaction, reducing cycle time and reducing defects.

The purpose of Six Sigma is to improve process capability, or reduce process variation, so that nearly all the products and services provided by an organisation meet or exceed customer expectations. The name derives from the use in statistics of the Greek character *sigma* (σ) as a measure of **standard deviation**: that is, how far a given process deviates from perfection. The higher the 'sigma number', the closer a process is to perfection.

The broad methodology of Six Sigma is as follows.

- Identify and prioritise characteristics that are 'critical to quality' (CTQ) for customers.
- Define detailed performance standards and tolerances for key variables.
- Statistically measure true process capability.

- Control defects and variations in the vital few factors.
- Involve management and staff in the process.

With regard to process improvement, Six Sigma uses a DMAIC (Define-Measure-Analyse-Improve-Control) methodology.

With regard to process design (or redesign), the DMADV (Define-Match/measure-Analyse-Design-Verify) model is used to achieve 'design for Six Sigma' (DfSS).

Creating continuous improvement

The Plan-Do-Check-Act (PDCA) cycle is a process improvement model that provides a structured framework for continuous improvement initiatives: it is also known as the **continuous improvement cycle**.

- Plan – plan ahead for change, and analyse and predict the results.
- Do – implement the solution, taking small steps in controlled circumstances.
- Check – measure the performance of the solution or impact of the change.
- Act – develop further action plans to standardise or improve the process.

The Japanese term *kaizen* is given to 'a Japanese concept of a total quality approach based on continual evolutionary change with considerable responsibility given to employees within certain fixed boundaries'. It is not so much 'get it right first time' as 'get it more right next time'.

Kaizen is also essentially a 'bottom up' approach to quality, because it utilises feedback, improvement suggestions and ideas from those closest to quality issues: operational staff and customers.

One technique for continuous improvement, utilised as part of TQM, is the use of 'quality circles' (also referred to as quality improvement teams or self-improvement study groups). This approach was pioneered in Japan in the 1960s by TQM guru Kaoru Ishikawa. It is based on recognition of the value of the worker, and reflects the principles of: participation management; human resource development; and problem-solving.

QCs are small voluntary-participation teams of employees from different levels and functions in an organisation (or representatives from the supply chain), which meet regularly to discuss issues relating to quality, share best practice and recommend improvements. QC activity is supported by a company-wide co-ordinator and administrative facilitators, often under the policy guidance of an executive steering committee. The activity of each QC is generally facilitated by a designated circle leader.

Sequence of QC activities:

- Problem identification, selection and analysis
- Development and evaluation of alternative solutions
- Developing an action plan for the developed solution
- Presenting the solution and action plan for approval and authorisation to proceed
- Implementation

Benefits of incremental improvement approaches:

- Build on existing skills, routines and beliefs in the organisation
- Allow flexibility and responsiveness to environmental changes and feedback
- Allow a continuous sense of progress, even through uncertainty and difficulty
- Empower employees

Own notes

CHAPTER 6

Developing Supply Chain Improvement

Just in time supply

Reasons for holding inventory:

- Reduces the risks of disruption to production from unforeseen events.
- Reduces the risks of disruption to production from long or uncertain delivery lead times.
- Allows rapid replenishment of goods which are in constant use and demand.
- Reduces the risk of stockouts.
- Buyers may be able to take advantage of bulk discounts, lower prices or reduced transaction costs.
- Buyers may be able to protect against anticipated shortages, price increases, or exchange rate fluctuations.
- Stocks of finished or almost-finished goods may be prepared ready for unexpected peaks in customer demand.
- Stocks of finished goods may be prepared during periods of slow demand.

However there are costs of acquiring stock and costs of holding stock. *Acquisition costs* decrease as inventory levels rise, because it is cheaper to make fewer, larger orders. But *holding costs* increase as inventory levels rise.

Techniques for efficient inventory management:

- Accurate demand forecasting through the supply chain
- Standardisation and variety reduction
- The use of systems contracts, call-off contracts, framework agreements etc
- The use of appropriate stock replenishment systems for independent demand items
- The use of appropriate 'pull' inventory management techniques for dependent demand items
- Just in time (JIT) supply

Two categories of inventory control: 'push' systems and 'pull' systems.

Just in time (JIT) supply aims to ensure that inputs only arrive at the factory (and particular work stations in the assembly line) 'just in time' to go into the production process. This is part of a broader management approach, based on eliminating process wastes and performing tasks only as and when required. The philosophy of JIT is that 'inventory is evil'.

Four key performance objectives: quality; speed; flexibility; dependability.

Elements of a just in time approach in practice.

- Reducing or eliminating inventory
- Reducing or eliminating quality defects
- Implementing preventive maintenance of plant and machinery
- Optimising process flows
- Continuous problem-solving and process improvement-seeking
- Developing and involving employees in process improvement (eg in quality circles)
- Supply chain collaboration and integration
- Improving visibility, order and cleanliness in workplace organisation

Business benefits of a JIT supply approach: more rapid stock turnover and reduced inventory costs; increase in ability to meet customer delivery promises; decreased delivery lead times; reduction in business waste; improved product and service quality; increased productivity; improved supply chain flexibility and responsiveness; resilience in the face of variable consumer demand.

Lean supply

'Lean production is "lean" because it uses less of every thing compared with mass production: half the human effort in the factory, half the factory space, half the investment in tools, half the engineering hours to develop a new product in half the time. Also, it requires far less than half of the needed inventory on site. The expected results are fewer defects, while producing a greater and ever growing variety of products' (Krafcik).

Five key principles to lean thinking:

- Specify what creates value as seen from the customer's perspective.
- Identify all steps across the value stream.
- Make actions that create value 'flow'.
- Only make what is pulled by customer demand, just in time.
- Strive for perfection by continually removing successive layers of waste.

Ohno's seven wastes: over-production; transportation; waiting; motion; over-processing; inventory; defects and corrections.

Lean production organisations exhibit certain structural and cultural features.

- Decentralisation of tasks and responsibilities to those who are actually adding value on the production line
- Control systems based on discovering defects and problems immediately, and eliminating their causes
- Comprehensive integrated information systems to enable swift and flexible response
- Horizontal organisation based on empowered cross-functional teams
- A strong sense of mutual loyalty between employees and the organisation
- Positive, clear communications

- A 'no blame' culture (to encourage initiative)
- A high degree of staff involvement
- The use of process maps to attract challenge and ideas
- An orientation to fixing root causes, not symptoms
- A philosophy of continuous improvement

One of the features of lean and just in time thinking is the 5S framework for good order and workplace organisation and cleanliness.

- *Shitsuke* – or Self-discipline
- *Seiri* – or Straighten: valuing tidiness
- *Seiton* – or Sort: establishing a state of orderliness
- *Seizo* – or Sweep: valuing cleanliness
- *Seiketsu* – or Standardise: specifically, standardising clean-up processes.

Benefits claimed for lean supply:

- The progressive removal of wastes, reducing costs and improving quality
- Closer collaborative relationships within the supply chain
- Cross-functional teamworking, involvement and flexibility
- Reduced inventories (also improving cashflow)
- Shorter cycle and delivery times
- More efficient process flows
- Fewer defects

Lean supply chains do, however, have their limitations – and are not suitable for all organisations in all circumstances.

Agile supply

The CIPS paper on lean and agile supply describes agile supply as 'using market knowledge and a responsive supply network to exploit profitable opportunities in the marketplace'. An agile organisation, for example, is better able to exploit opportunities for product modification at any time that the market appears ready for it. Achieving agility requires:

- Streamlining the physical flow of parts from suppliers
- Streamlining and synchronising the flow of information
- Adaptability in responding to changing needs of the market
- Measuring the performance of the supply chain using suitable agility metrics.

Agile is different from lean in that it embraces the philosophy and takes the advantages of lean, but seeks to build on them by offering more flexibility, built in at the strategic level. Manufacturing will be able to be more responsive, products will go from design to market more quickly, the expertise of the supply network will be more fully utilised – and change will be an accepted part of the operation.

Lean philosophy is most powerful when the winning criteria are cost and quality. Agility is paramount where service and customer value enhancement are key.

Whereas lean thinking attempts to remove stock from the supply chain, as being a source of waste, agile thinking is more ready to accept stock, provided the reasons for holding it are sound. One example is a supplier who is asked by customers to hold stock to enable response on very short lead times. This is an example where stock is not a source of cost, but of value enhancement for the customer. Another example is the holding of stocks of work in progress, waiting to be converted into finished goods in response to customer orders ('late customisation').

Another distinction between lean and agile is based on how manufacturing companies supply their customers.

- Lean manufacturing aims to produce goods only when 'pulled' by a customer (just in time) and to the standard of quality required by the customer.
- Agile manufacturing goes one step further, by means of 'late customisation': aiming to *finish or assemble* goods in rapid response to customer orders, and to the specification of the customer.

Improvement priorities and trade-offs

Trade-offs must often be made between the four basic manufacturing capabilities.

- Quality
- Dependability (of the manufacturing and supply process)
- Speed (flexibility and speed of response to changing demands)
- Cost

Unless there is some slack in the system, improving any one of these variables will necessarily be at the expense of one (or more) of the other three. Increasing speed, for example, usually means increasing cost.

The sand cone model argues that, although in the short term it is possible to trade off manufacturing capabilities against each other, there is in fact a hierarchy of priority among the four capabilities. In order to build long-term cumulative, lasting and competitive manufacturing capability:

- Attention must be given to developing capabilities in a particular sequence
- Capabilities should be considered as cumulative developments, building on one another – rather than trading off against each other.

The analogy is one of building up a cone or 'pile' of grains of sand. To build a stable sand cone, the base must be continually widened, in order to support the increasing height of the cone – otherwise it will collapse.

Business process re-engineering

Hammer and Champy pioneered the concept of business process re-engineering (BPR) as: 'The fundamental rethinking and radical redesign of business processes to achieve dramatic improvements in critical, contemporary measures of performance, such as cost, quality, service and speed'.

BPR uses a 'blank sheet of paper' approach. Re-engineers start with the future – what they want to achieve – and work backwards, unconstrained by existing assumptions, methods, people or structures.

Both total quality management and BPR are concerned with improving business processes to support greater customer value and competitive advantage. However, TQM is a process of continuous incremental improvement. BPR contrasts with this approach in several key respects.

- BRP is a 'discontinuous' change and improvement process.
- BRP is a technique of radical, revolutionary or 'transformational' change.
- As a technique of revolutionary change, BPR is often a reactive approach.
- BPR is time bounded, as a discrete change programme.
- BPR is an explicitly strategic process which can only be implemented from the 'top down'.

The MOST framework for BPR: management; organisation; social systems; technology.

Benefits of BPR:

- Breakthrough improvement – BPR helps organisations take a more radical approach to quality and competitive advantage
- Organisational structure – a genuine focus on the efficient flow of value to the customer
- Corporate culture – empowering workers to take ownership of process performance
- Job redesign – more satisfying, integrated roles, with resulting gains in both performance and employee/partner commitment

However, BPR has gained a poor reputation over the years, partly because of its early application with a focus on cost reduction (and resulting corporate down-sizing). Moreover, failure rates for BPR projects are put as high as 70%, attributed to factors such as lack of senior management understanding and support, unrealistic expectations, and resistance to change.

Benchmarking in supply chains

Benchmarking is: 'Measuring your performance against that of best-in-class companies, determining how the best-in-class achieve these performance levels and using the information as a basis for your own company's targets, strategies and implementation'. The aim is to learn both *where* performance needs to be improved and *how* it can be improved, by comparison with excellent practitioners.

Four types of benchmarking:

- *Internal benchmarking*
- *Competitor benchmarking*
- *Functional benchmarking*
- *Generic benchmarking*

Stages in the benchmarking process: plan; data collection and analysis; develop; improve; review.

The SCOR model was developed as a standard diagnostic tool for supply chain management, covering process modelling, performance measurement and best practice. The process model sets out five basic management processes: planning, sourcing, making, delivering and returning (reverse logistics).

Potential advantages of using benchmarking techniques:

- Developing a more comprehensive understanding about the process being analysed, especially relating to cost and performance
- Moving the organisation from 'compliance'-based quality systems to performance-based evaluations, reflecting the pursuit of added value and competitive advantage
- Replacing an *ad hoc* or subjective approach to improvement and competition with a set of objective, systematic criteria
- Raising awareness of changing customer needs and expectations
- Encouraging innovative thinking for process improvement
- Establishing realistic but stretching goals and action plans for process improvement

Whilst benchmarking can make significant contributions to continuous improvement objectives, the following points should also be considered.

- The costs associated with benchmarking projects are variable, but can be significant.
- Benchmarking can be counter-productive, if it is met with defensive attitudes and resistance.
- Commercially sensitive benchmarking data can be difficult to obtain ethically.
- Benchmarking cannot be a one-off process.

Own notes

Own notes

CHAPTER 7

Pursuing Competitive Advantage

Competitive strategy

A business can achieve competitive advantage by performing strategically important activities more cheaply or better than its competitors. Success in securing competitive advantage – or successful competition – is measured mainly by **market share**.

Porter's generic strategies for competitive advantage

COMPETITIVE SCOPE	COMPETITIVE ADVANTAGE: *Lower cost*	COMPETITIVE ADVANTAGE: *Differentiation*
Broad (industry wide)	Cost leadership	Differentiation
Narrow (market segment)	Cost focus	Differentiation focus

Cost leadership is the key source of competitive advantage for organisations competing in a price-sensitive market. Pursuing an overall cost leadership strategy will require a firm to adopt tactics such as: large-scale production to secure economies of scale ('high-volume, low-cost'); enhancing productivity through technology; seeking continuous improvement and waste reduction; and minimising supply and materials handling costs.

From a supply chain perspective, the major implication of a cost leadership strategy is the emphasis on cost reduction, through measures such as inventory minimisation, robust requirements and transport planning, variety reduction and quality control, transaction streamlining, price negotiation, aggregation of requirements, supply base rationalisation and so on.

Differentiation is a key source of competitive advantage for an organisation faced by a strong low-cost competitor. The strategy is to gain advantage by differentiating the product from lower-priced ones on the basis of some non-price factor: in other words, setting it apart in customers' minds. From a supply chain perspective, a differentiation strategy permits, encourages – and arguably, requires – closer collaborative relationships with suppliers.

Innovation capability and leadership supports differentiation through: technology leverage; excellent product functionality and design; unique product features; continually 'new', adapting and improving features; and a loyal brand following among early adopters and style leaders.

Customer care may likewise be a source of differentiation in a range of ways.

Relationship advantage

Two views of competitive strategy

- A **positioning-based approach** to strategy suggests that the source of an organisation's competitive advantage is mainly in how it achieves strategic 'fit' with its external environment, exploiting opportunities and minimising threats.
- The **resource-based approach** suggests that the source of an organisation's competitive advantage lies mainly in how it exploits its distinctive internal resources and competencies, setting strategic objectives based on what they enable it to do.

Competencies are 'the activities or processes through which the organisation deploys its resources effectively' (Johnson, Scholes and Whittington).

- **Threshold** competencies are the basic capabilities necessary to support a particular strategy or to enable the organisation to compete in a given market.
- **Core** competencies are distinctive value-creating skills, capabilities and resources which add value in the eyes of the customer; are scarce and difficult for competitors to imitate; and are flexible for future needs.

Porter's generic competitive strategies are essentially based on a positioning approach. However, some have argued that competitive advantage based on positioning is not sustainable in the long term.

High-quality, motivated and committed suppliers have the potential to contribute significantly to a business in many areas.

- New product development and process innovation
- Availability and delivery
- Quality
- Value for money
- Service, advice and information

Benefits of positive supplier relationship management:

- Stronger relationships
- Sound risk management
- Better return on relationship investment
- Improved business efficiency
- Greater profitability
- Potential for value-adding synergy
- Improved corporate social responsibility and reputation management
- Competitive advantage

Circumstances where suppliers are strategic:

- If they supply items which are strategic or critical to the effective performance of business processes, or to the buyer's product and brand
- If there are few alternative sources of supply for critical items
- If they supply rare, distinctive, hard-to-imitate, value-adding competencies
- If contracts with them represent a significant proportion of the buying organisation's external spend
- If their resources and competencies mitigate significant downside supply risks
- If there is potential for significant synergy
- If significant investment has already been made

Circumstances where suppliers are tactical or operational:

- If they supply items which are routine and/or non-critical to business processes
- If there are multiple suppliers in the market
- If they are unable to offer any unique, value-adding, competitive competencies

Prioritising supply chain relationships

Portfolio analysis and supplier segmentation involve categorising and dividing the firm's supplies and/or suppliers into different classes, according to relevant criteria such as volume and value of business, profitability, supply risk – or, broadly, 'importance' to the firm's strategic objectives. The segment into which a given supply or supplier falls indicates the purchasing resources, sourcing approach and relationship type that will be most important, as a basis for strategic relationship management.

Tools of segmentation:

- Risk identification and assessment
- Portfolio analysis (eg the Kraljic matrix)
- Supplier preferencing

A simple **risk assessment** can be performed by using a matrix on which procurements, suppliers or risk factors can be plotted according to probability and impact.

The **Kraljic matrix** maps two factors: the importance of the item being purchased and the complexity of the supply market.

- For **non-critical or routine items** (such as common stationery supplies), the focus will be on low-maintenance routines to reduce procurement costs.
- For **bottleneck items** (such as proprietary spare parts or specialised consultancy services, which could cause operational delays if unavailable), the buyer's priority will be ensuring control over the continuity and security of supply.
- For **leverage items** (such as local produce bought by a major supermarket), the buyer's priority will be to use its dominance to secure best prices and terms, on a purely transactional basis.
- For **strategic items** (such as key subassemblies bought by a car manufacturer, or Intel processors bought by laptop manufacturers), there is likely to be mutual dependency

and investment, and the focus will be on the total cost, security and competitiveness of supply.

The **supplier preferencing model** is another matrix, this time illustrating how attractive it is to a supplier to deal with a buyer, and the monetary value of the buyer's business to the supplier.

A buying firm may become less attractive to suppliers in any of the following situations.

- It often makes late payments, or negotiates highly unfavourable terms.
- It constantly queries, changes or disputes order details and terms.
- It uses (and demands) excessive red tape or bureaucracy.
- It has a bad reputation (in regard to ethical dealings, labour standards, customer service or product safety, say).
- It is excessively litigious.

Such a customer might suffer the penalties of such conduct, and poor relationship management.

The relationship lifecycle

Like organisms, relationships can be seen as progressing through lifecycle stages of birth, growth, maturity, decline and death.

Lifecycle models draw attention to helpful questions such as these.

- Where in the lifecycle is the relationship with a given supplier or client?
- Where *should* it be, in light of the type of purchase (eg using the Kraljic matrix) – and how can this be managed?
- What risks and conflicts of interest are likely to arise at each stage of the cycle, and how can they be managed?
- What opportunities for competitive advantage are presented at each stage?

However, such models represent an ideal linear progression. In practice, relationships ebb and flow.

Developing supplier relationships

Supplier approval is: 'the recognition, following a process of appraisal, that a particular supplier is able to meet the standards and requirements of the particular buyer. The approval may be for a one-off transaction or mean that the supplier is put on a list of approved suppliers'. New suppliers will have to be supported through the early stages of the relationship.

Successfully managing the shift towards long-term partnership relations may require the consideration of factors such as the following.

- Monitoring and managing risks of being 'locked into' longer-term ties
- Improving communication at all levels

- Implementing or improving performance measurement
- Ensuring strategic as well as operational 'fit' between the organisations
- Monitoring 'trade-offs' in the objectives of the alliance

Buyers can motivate suppliers by offering incentives for them to perform to the required standard, or to improve their level of service, or to add value in some other way. Alternatively, they can penalise suppliers for poor performance.

Examples of supplier incentives:

- Staged payments or contingency payments
- Specific key performance indicators (KPIs) or improvement targets linked to recognition and rewards
- Revenue, profit or gain sharing
- The promise of long-term business agreements or increased business, or the award of 'preferred supplier' status
- Guaranteed or fixed order levels
- Opportunities for innovation
- A capped price for the product or service that decreases year on year
- The offer of development support
- Supplier award programmes
- Positive feedback sharing, praise and thanks from the buying team

Here are some potential **sanctions or penalties**.

- The threat of reduced business for poor performance
- The threat of removal from the approved or preferred supplier list
- Publicised poor supplier gradings ('name and shame')
- Penalty clauses in contracts

While penalties support compliance with minimum standards of performance, they usually encourage only short-term improvements at best. Fundamental issues are often not addressed, and the relationship invariably suffers. The 'carrot' is generally acknowledged to be more effective than the 'stick' where the aim is long-term commitment, co-operation and improvement.

Six key elements to developing **high-trust supplier relationships**

- Model the behaviours you expect.
- Keep and exceed commitments.
- Proactively develop trust.
- Disclose information.
- Measure trust.
- Be empathetic.

There are many approaches to the management of **conflict**, and the suitability of any given approach must be judged according to its relevance to a particular situation. There is no single 'right way'. In some situations, the best outcome may be achieved by compromise; in others, imposition of a win-lose solution may be required; in others, the process of seeking a win-win solution, whatever the eventual outcome, may be helpful – particularly where the parties want to preserve ongoing working relations.

Key issues in terminating a supply relationship:

- Timing
- Relationship aspects
- Legal considerations
- Succession issues

Creating partnership sourcing arrangements

Steps in setting up a partnership relationship:

- Step 1 Which markets and which products and services?
- Step 2 Sell the idea
- Step 3 Choose your partners
- Step 4 Define what you want from the partnership relationship
- Step 5 Make your first partnering relationship work
- Step 6 Refine and develop

Checklist for organisations wishing to establish partnership sourcing:

- Has the organisation signalled a willingness or commitment to a partnership-type arrangement?
- Is the organisation willing to commit resources that it cannot use in other relationships?
- How early in the product design stage is the organisation willing or able to participate?
- What does the organisation bring to the relationship that is unique?
- Will the organisation have a genuine interest in joint problem solving and a win-win agreement?
- Is the organisation's senior management committed to the process inherent in strategic partnerships?
- Will there be free and open exchange of information across functional areas between companies?
- Does the organisation have the infrastructure to support such cross-functional interdependence?
- How much future planning is the organisation willing to share with us?
- Is the need for confidential treatment taken seriously?
- What is the general level of comfort between companies?
- How well does the organisation know our business?
- Will the organisation share cost data?
- What will be the organisation's commitment to understanding our problems and concerns?
- Will we be special to the organisation or just another customer or supplier?

Factors constraining relationship development:

- Lack of support from senior managers in the organisation
- Conflicts of interest between the two parties
- An adversarial approach on the part of a buyer or supplier
- Imbalance of power between the parties
- Lack of trust
- Changes of personnel
- Communication breakdown
- Dissatisfaction, conflict and lack of trust arising from repeated failure to meet agreed terms
- Incompatibility of culture and values, processes and procedures, or systems and technology
- Commercial factors

Own notes

CHAPTER 8

Pursuing Cost Advantage

Cost and price analysis

The **price** of a procurement is what a supplier charges for the package of benefits offered to a buyer. The **cost** of a procurement properly includes all the finance and resources expended to acquire, transport, install, maintain, operate, insure and dispose of procured items.

Price management involves a buying organisation managing or reducing its **input costs** by ensuring that it secures the **optimum price** for routine and leverage procurements (for which competitive purchase price – rather than whole-life value for money – is the priority).

- **Price analysis** is the process of seeking to determine if the price offered is a fair and appropriate price for the goods.
- **Cost analysis** is often used to support price negotiations where the supplier justifies its price by the need to cover its costs.

It is important to allow suppliers to make a reasonable profit:

- In order to protect the security of supply
- In order to protect the quality of supply
- In the interests of responsible procurement and sustainability

Suppliers may be asked to include cost breakdowns with their price quotations. In a close, long-term supply relationship, there may be a policy of:

- **Open book costing**, where suppliers provide information about their costs to buyers
- **Cost transparency**, where both buyer and supplier share cost information

In open book costing, buyer and supplier work together to understand their respective costs. Both parties are able to see a breakdown of the supplier's costs, with a view to negotiating an agreed supply cost structure and profit margin.

It is useful to know a supplier's cost structure:

- Cost analysis can be used to keep prices realistic.
- It focuses attention on what costs *ought* to be involved.
- It identifies the minimum price the supplier can afford to charge for *sustainable* supply.
- It enables the buyer to estimate how valuable the business or contract will be to the supplier.

Possible ethical and sustainability issues in open book costing:

- Open book costing is often used as a tool to 'squeeze' or leverage supplier prices.
- Open book costing is generally only a 'one way street'.
- The added value gains from open book costing may not be equitably shared with suppliers.

Open book costing *can,* however, be used responsibly to support a sustainable procurement agenda.

Cost transparency is not widely adopted in current practice, as there is a strongly embedded tendency for managers to want to protect 'sensitive' information such as profit margins and technical details. However, transparency should gain greater acceptance where strategic collaborative supply chain relationships continue to develop.

Pricing arrangements

Four types of pricing arrangements:

- Fixed pricing
- Variable pricing
- Incentivised pricing
- Cost-plus pricing

When is firm pricing suitable?

- A reasonably comprehensive and accurate specification is available.
- Fair prices can be estimated more or less accurately.
- There is relatively little risk of cost variation.
- Electronic purchase to pay systems are utilised.

Firm fixed price agreements are advantageous to the buyer, in terms of: financial risk; cashflow management; supplier motivation; administrative simplicity.

In order to maintain the security of supply and a sustainable and equitable supply relationship, it is often seen as desirable to reduce the financial risks to both buyer (on the basis of a cost-plus agreement) and supplier (on the basis of a firm price agreement). This can be done by incorporating variations – allowing flexibility – into a firm pricing arrangement. Techniques include use of appropriate indices, CPA clauses, or contract review clauses.

Under a **cost-plus** arrangement, the buyer agrees to reimburse the supplier for all allowable, allocable (ie directly attributable to the work undertaken for the buyer) and reasonable costs incurred in performing the contract *plus* a fixed fee or percentage representing the supplier's profit. Variations include: cost plus fixed fee; cost without fee; cost sharing; time and materials contracts.

Cost-plus arrangements are disadvantageous to the buyer, in terms of: financial risk; supplier motivation; administration and contract management costs.

Target costing differs considerably from the cost-plus approach.

- The cost-plus approach builds up the cost of a product by analysing its components step by step. A profit margin is then added and the result is the selling price of the product.
- A target costing approach starts at the other end. The supplier estimates the maximum selling price that the market will be willing to pay for a product with specific features, or negotiates a maximum price (including an agreed profit) with a particular buyer. It then works backwards to calculate the production cost that must be achieved in order to provide a reasonable profit, and attacks costs to reduce them to the required level.

In a **target price** arrangement, the contract stipulates a *target price* (based on target cost, including an agreed profit margin) and a *maximum or ceiling price* for the contract. Any excess costs, over and above the maximum price, are borne by the supplier. Any cost savings, below the target cost, are shared on an agreed percentage basis, between the supplier and the buyer.

This is essentially a form of fixed price incentive contract. It may be suitable where:

- Target cost can be determined with a reasonable degree of accuracy and certainty *but*
- Exact total costs cannot be accurately forecast at the time of the contract *and*
- The buyer has the power to negotiate a position in which it does not have to bear the risk of extra costs.

Supplier incentives

A fixed or cost-plus price arrangement may provide for adjustment of the final price to include various supplier incentives: additional 'bonus' payments, profit allowances or value gain sharing, as an incentive for the supplier to shorten lead times or deliver on time, improve quality or technical performance, or – most relevant to the focus of this chapter – achieve cost savings.

Options for incentivisation in pricing and gainshare mechanisms: 8

- **Staged payments**
- The establishment of a negotiated **target cost** for supply, on which a fixed maximum price (including a 'target profit' for the supplier) is based.
- Specified bonus payments (or **incentive fees**) added to the fixed price, linked to attainment of specific KPIs.
- A **cost plus incentive fee (CPIF)** arrangement
- A **cost plus award fee (CPAF)** arrangement
- Revenue, profit or gain sharing
- A fixed price for the product or service that *decreases* year on year through the contract, motivating the supplier progressively to improve efficiency

In an incentive contract based on cost targets or reductions, the cost responsibility is shared by the buyer and supplier. As well as motivating the supplier to control costs, this may prevent the supplier from inflating or 'padding' the contract price to minimise the risks of cost uncertainty.

Gainsharing is a negotiated approach offering specific financial incentives for suppliers to achieve cost reductions. A gainsharing clause in a contract allows the supplier to retain a defined portion of any cost reduction initiative that positively impacts the customer. From the buyer's perspective, this form of incentivisation is achieved 'free of charge': the payment of incentive awards to the supplier is made from savings created by supplier innovations or excellent cost management.

Risk/reward mechanisms are intended to give a contractor a meaningful stake in the outcome of a project, in the meeting of objectives, and in the management of risks and costs. Anywhere from 10–40% of the total value of a contract may be made part of the risk/reward element: contingent upon the contractor meeting defined KPIs and objectives for cost and budget, key milestone dates and completion date.

Cost reduction activities

The reduction and management of costs will be a key objective to support the financial objectives of the firm. A five-step generic approach may be used in the management of procurement and supply chain cost reduction activities: understand the drivers for reducing costs; understand why excess costs exist in the supply chain; focus and prioritise cost-down initiatives; develop appropriate strategies and tactics; review and measure performance.

Short-term cost elimination or reduction options:

- Challenging internal customer requisitions and specifications
- Improving the accuracy of demand forecasting
- Controlling 'maverick' buying by users
- Consolidating or aggregating requirements
- Negotiating 'harder' for reductions in prices and costs
- Proactive sourcing
- Utilising available technology tools more effectively
- Operating tendering and contracting processes more efficiently
- Reducing costs of quality failure
- Using value analysis
- Considering the use of international (particularly low-cost country) suppliers

Longer-term strategic cost reduction options:

- Restructuring: delayering, downsizing or horizontalising purchasing structures
- Centralising procurement *or* decentralising procurement
- Process engineering or re-engineering
- Applying ICT and automation technologies to streamline processes
- Developing collaborative supply relationships for cost and price advantages
- Rationalising the supplier base
- Developing lean supply and production
- Collaborating with key supply chain partners on cost reduction programmes
- Investigating the potential for global and low-cost country sourcing
- Considering the outsourcing (or offshoring) of non-core activities

It is increasingly recognised that collaborative approaches to supply are more effective in securing long-term, sustainable, value-adding price and cost reductions.

- Cost reduction opportunities are not confined to the buyer or supplier organisation, but arise from their interaction or 'linkages' in the value chain.
- Collaborative approaches seek to secure end-to-end supply chain cost reductions.
- Techniques such as target costing, open book costing and cost transparency depend on close co-operation and trust.
- Cost reduction approaches such as lean supply, supply base rationalisation, etc all depend on the development of close, trusting, long-term relationships.

'Squeezing' suppliers in hard-bargaining price negotiation is the traditional competitive approach to tactical cost reduction: effectively, making the reduction of a quoted or contracted price, by an agreed amount, the condition for winning or retaining a contract. This approach may secure short-term cost reductions, where this is a priority.

- It may be the optimal approach for 'leverage' or 'tactical profit' procurements.
- It may be specifically indicated where the buyer has reason to believe that a supplier is growing complacent about cost management.

However, adversarial negotiation is likely to be counter-productive in the long term.

- Increased sustainability risk and resulting reputational risk
- Lower levels of service and quality

Supply base optimisation

One approach to managing supply risk is by having *more* potential suppliers of a given item or category of purchases, pre-qualified and approved as being able to meet requirements. However, there are key disadvantages of multiple sourcing arrangements.

- They can lead to unnecessarily high procurement costs.
- They fail to exploit the value-adding and competitive potential of collaborative relationships with fewer suppliers.
- They can lead to waste.

Commonly, therefore, strong collaborative supplier relationships are used to 'narrow supply', enabling purchases to be concentrated on a smaller group of developed and trusted supply partners.

Circumstances for **single sourcing**:

- The total requirement is too small to justify splitting orders.
- One supplier is far ahead of others in terms of reputation, quality, price etc.
- Expensive set-up costs are required to enable supply.
- The requirement is subject to supply risk, or in short supply.
- The buyer hopes to gain supplier commitment and co-investment.

Slightly less risky is **dual sourcing.**

Supplier complacency is a key issue in both single and dual sourcing.

Supply base rationalisation is the process of optimising the number of suppliers the organisation deals with. This is mainly a process of reduction or consolidation. This contributes to cost advantage in the following ways.

- Reducing market engagement, sourcing and transaction costs
- Reducing supplier management costs
- Freeing up procurement capability for strategic cost reduction activities
- Leveraging supplier relationships and capabilities
- Rewarding the best suppliers with extra business
- Supporting the aggregation of requirements

Five stages in supplier rationalisation: supplier analysis and segmentation; establish evaluation criteria; supplier evaluation; supplier selection; implementation plan.

Disadvantages of supplier rationalisation:

- Increasing dependency on suppliers, and resulting exposure to supplier and supply risk
- Reduced competitiveness of supply, due to supplier complacency
- Reduced capacity for supply innovation

Advantages of aggregating requirements:

- Economies of scale
- Volume-related price advantages
- Volume-related bargaining power for the buyer
- The ability to rationalise the supplier base

A **buying consortium** is a group of separate organisations that combine together for the purpose of procuring goods or services. Benefits:

- The consortium can obtain discounts that would not be available to individual members.
- A consortium can establish framework agreements.
- Consortium members can pool expertise, knowledge and contacts.

Disadvantages of a buying consortium:

- There are costs and effort associated with communication and coordination.
- There is an issue of transparency between consortium members.
- Consortia may suffer from lengthy negotiation and decision processes.
- Members are not obliged to purchase to the agreed specification.
- Very large consortia may fall foul of laws and regulations.

Two methods of minimising stock proliferation:

- **Standardisation** involves agreeing and adopting generic specifications or descriptions of the items required.
- **Variety reduction** is a systematic rationalisation or reduction in the range of items used, stocked, bought or made.

This offers potential for efficiencies and cost savings in several areas: specification; purchasing; transport; inventory; quality management.

Value analysis and value engineering

Value analysis is 'the organised, systematic study of the function of a material, part, component or system to identify areas of unnecessary cost. It begins with the question "What is it worth?" and proceeds to an analysis of value in terms of the function the item performs'.

The approach is summarised in five 'tests for value'.

- Does use of the material, part or process contribute value?
- Is the cost of the material, part or process proportionate to its usefulness?
- Are all the product features actually needed?
- Can a lower-cost method be used while retaining the features and functions that add value?
- Is anyone paying less for this part?

A helpful mnemonic is STOPS WASTE:

- **S**tandardisation
- **T**ransportation classification
- **O**ver-engineering
- **P**ackaging
- **S**ubstitute goods or components
- **W**eight reduction
- **A**ny unnecessary processing
- **S**upplier's input
- **T**o make rather than buy
- **E**liminate waste, obsolescence, redundancy

Four main phases in value analysis:

- Information: defining the problem to be solved
- Speculation: using functional analysis systems technique (FAST)
- Analysis
- Proposal

The term 'value engineering' is generally used more specifically for the application of value analysis *from the product design and development stage onwards*. It involves cross-functional teams in this process, including specialists from all the functions that can contribute to overall objectives, and external suppliers.

Own notes

CHAPTER 9

Collaborative Improvement and Innovation

Cross-functional working

In a 'functional' organisation structure, tasks are grouped together according to the common nature or focus of the task: production, sales and marketing, accounting and finance, procurement and so on. This enables cost-effective use of specialist expertise and related resources. Unfortunately, it can also create barriers between different functions: information and work flows are primarily 'vertical' within functions, which may be seen as separate 'silos' within the organisation.

Drivers of cross-functional teamworking in procurement:

- The increasing involvement of procurement staff in strategic decisions
- The increasing adoption of a supply chain philosophy
- Its ability to make best use of developments in ICT
- The adoption of advanced world class systems
- The increasing complexity and dynamism of global markets and technologies
- The need to leverage human resource capability

Different forms of cross-functional teams:

- Multi-functional or multi-disciplinary teams
- Multi-skilled teams
- Project teams and task forces
- Virtual teams

Cross-functional procurement teams are particularly valuable in increasing team members' awareness of the big picture and process focus of their tasks and decisions – and therefore dovetailing functional objectives and agendas with the overall objectives of the organisation or project.

Potential downsides to cross-functional team or project working:

- It adds potential for time-consuming complexity, conflict and consensus-seeking.
- It may lack clear lines of authority.
- There may be difficulties of dual authority structures.
- All teams take time to develop before they perform effectively.

- There may be practical difficulties of organising meetings and information flows.
- Teams may themselves become mini 'silos'.

In developing specifications, procurement can contribute: supply market awareness; supplier contacts; awareness of commercial aspects; awareness of legal aspects; procurement disciplines.

Cross-functional input to design and development

Early supplier involvement (ESI) is: 'A practice that brings together one or more selected suppliers with a buyer's product design team early in the product development process. The objective is to utilise the supplier's expertise and experience in developing a product specification that is designed for effective and efficient product roll-out.'

Supplier contributions to the product development process:

- Constructive criticism of designs
- Technical information
- Supply market information

Advantages and disadvantages of ESI

ADVANTAGES OF ESI	DISADVANTAGES/PROBLEMS OF ESI
Quicker development lead time to bring a concept to the market	Longer development lead time, if the process is conflicted or inefficient
Improved product specifications and improved manufacturability of products	Heavy investment in inter-company communication
Enhanced quality and lower development costs	May get 'trapped' with incompatible supplier because of co-investment in R & D
Access to new technologies ahead of competitors	Potential for conflict from different goals and agendas
Shared expertise for problem-solving	Risk if supplier or technology is unfamiliar
Exchange of knowledge and information, building trust and alliance: making the supplier feel part of the organisation 'team'	Risk of leakage of information and intellectual property (especially if ESI suppliers become, or serve, competitors)
Improved understanding of supplier capabilities, with potential for future development and partnership	Risk if products or services are designed around the supplier (dependency)

Simultaneous engineering attempts to organise the design and development of new products or services by using cross-functional teams, including specialists from all the functions that can contribute to overall objectives, as well as external suppliers.

Quality function deployment (QFD) uses a similar cross-functional approach. Customer research is carried out among both internal and external customers, and their core requirements must be satisfied before any product or service design can be regarded as complete. This ensures that any given design is marketable, correctly specified – and achievable in production.

Promoting supply chain innovation

Innovation has been defined simply as 'the successful exploitation of new ideas'. Schumpeter distinguished three stages in the process by which new ideas develop and become adopted by an industry or market.

- Invention
- Innovation
- Diffusion

Forms of supply innovation:

- Development and application of new products, processes, and services to satisfy previously unmet market needs
- Development and application of new products, processes, and services to serve existing market needs.
- Use of existing products, processes, and services in new applications
- Incremental improvements to existing products, processes, and services for their existing applications

Incremental innovation develops in an evolutionary manner. 'Most companies are built for continuous improvement, rather than for discontinuous innovation. They know how to get better – but they don't know how to get different.'

The term **discontinuous or breakthrough innovation** is used to describe innovations that radically transform or revolutionise processes, leading to breakthrough value creation along the supply chain.

Forward commitment procurement (FCP) is 'a commitment to purchase, at a point in the future, a product that does not yet exist commercially, against a specification that current products do not meet, at a sufficient scale to make it worthwhile for suppliers to invest in tooling up and manufacture'.

'Thinking differently' about SCM:

- The 'old' approach to supply chains is based on **linear thinking**, where relationships are seen only in terms of immediate upstream and downstream links.
- A newer approach is **network thinking**.
- The emergent – or innovative – supply chain approach involves **systems thinking**.

Problems with innovation:

- It is difficult for top management to develop a clear overview of the levels of activity and resource investment, creating a lack of innovation visibility.
- Initiatives may be pursued in a fragmented and uncoordinated manner.
- Initiatives may be 'well intentioned' – but *ad hoc*.
- There is a resulting waste of expenditures of time, money and human capital.

In response to these issues, innovation councils are increasingly used by larger organisations, as a mechanism to coordinate and manage the business innovation process. An innovation council is a small, cross-functional team of senior managers which oversees and directs innovation management activities across the business.

Roles of the innovation council:

- To ensure that innovation-related activities are coordinated across the organisation
- To ensure that any innovation activity is in alignment with business objectives
- To ensure that innovation initiatives are supported by appropriate processes and resources
- To resolve any business barriers to innovation activities
- To provide a governance structure and executive sponsorship

Supply chain managers can also encourage collaborative innovation-seeking and problem-solving in the wider supply network, by encouraging the use of **supplier forums** or the formation of a **supplier association**.

A **knowledge community** is a group of individuals or organisations with a common interest, and a willingness to share ideas and experience. A knowledge community may exist within a single organisation. Alternatively, a knowledge community could involve a wide range of individuals and organisations, facilitated by ICT networks such as the internet. The term **communities of practice** (COP) is often given to groups of people drawn together to facilitate learning and best practice sharing *other than* with immediate work colleagues.

Technology transfer

Technology transfer may take place in a variety of ways. Individual trading partners may supply their subsidiaries, suppliers or joint venture partners in developing nations with any of: technological knowledge, management expertise, consultancy and training; investment for new technology; access to design patents; finished technology products.

Drawbacks of technology:

- High capital investment and set-up costs
- High initial learning curve costs
- Reliability issues, especially at an early stage of development
- Compatibility issues
- The pace of technological development varies from economy to economy
- There may also be ethical issues in the adoption of technology by a business

Supplier development

Supplier development is: 'Any activity that a buyer undertakes to improve a supplier's performance and/or capabilities to meet the buyer's short-term or long-term supply needs'.

Responsibilities and roles in supplier development can be structured in various ways.

- Supplier development programmes will often involve **cross-functional representatives** from both buyer and supplier organisations.
- In addition, communication systems will probably provide for **multiple contact points** in both organisations, for ongoing monitoring and management.
- Another common practice is the temporary **transfer of staff**.

To further reinforce the interface with key suppliers some organisations have introduced the role of **executive sponsors**. Main responsibilities for the executive sponsor:

- Coordinate internal and external interactions with key supplier.
- Ensure the alignment of organisational strategic objectives with supplier development objectives.
- Promote relational alliance within both buyer and supplier organisations.
- Review achievements.
- Resolve relational barriers.
- Input suggestions and recommendations for future supplier relational enhancements.

Two generic approaches to supplier development programmes: directive and facilitative.

A wide variety of approaches may be used to bridge perceived performance or relationship gaps. Here are some examples.

- Enhancing working relationships (eg by improved communication systems and routines)
- Clarifying or increasing performance goals and measures
- Seconding purchaser's staff to the supplier
- Providing capital
- Providing progress payments during the development of a project or product
- Loaning machinery, equipment or IT hardware
- Granting access to IT and ICT systems and information
- Using the purchaser's bargaining power to obtain materials or equipment for the supplier at a discount
- Offering training for the supplier's staff
- Providing help or consultancy on value analysis (waste reduction) programmes, costing or other areas of expertise
- Encouraging the formation of supplier forums or a supplier association

Own notes

CHAPTER 10

Technology Tools

Technology and supply chain improvement

Developments in ICT and automation:

- Opening up new supply markets
- Changing business processes
- Raising supply chain capacity and productivity
- Improving communication and the visibility of information
- Changing the way that supply chains are organised and managed
- Offering opportunities for cost reductions
- Freeing up procurement professionals' time
- Enhancing management information and feedback
- Supporting the development of supply chain relationships
- Reducing the risk of fraud

The development of procurement systems

- **Independence:** procurement operates within its own guidelines, with a focus on functional efficiencies and improvements.
- **Dependence:** procurement dovetails with other functions via consultation and reporting, but still uses a standalone information system.
- **Business integration:** procurement systematically integrates with other functions in the internal supply chain.
- **Chain integration:** procurement has a key role in securing systematic co-operation and information-sharing across the supply chain.

E-procurement and e-sourcing

The term e-procurement (or e-purchasing) may be used as an umbrella term for 'the combined use of information and communication technology through electronic means to enhance external and internal purchasing and supply management processes'.

A broad ranging e-procurement and e-sourcing system allows procurement staff to perform the following tasks: identifying and defining needs; sourcing the market; purchase to pay and contract management.

Activities in inventory management:

- Demand management
- Forecasting demand (and therefore supply requirements) in order to avoid over-stocking
- Controlling stock levels
- Ensuring that supplies are replenished in accordance with procurement policies
- Developing cost-effective systems and procedures for ordering and procurement of supplies
- Controlling the receipt, inspection, storage and issuing of supplies to users
- Ensuring that stocks are safe and secure from deterioration, damage, theft or obsolescence.

Electronic systems can support a number of these activities, via technologies for:

- Data capture
- Inventory control and information systems
- Warehouse management systems.

RFID offers significant advantages, compared to conventional optical scanning of barcodes.

- The tag doesn't have to be scanned or 'seen' by the reader.
- Data can be flexibly interrogated and updated.
- A *CIPS Practice Guide* argues that RFID can offer improved product availability; improved utilisation of resources; lower total operating costs; and enhanced safety, security and quality control.

Examples of requirement planning and specification tools:

- Integrated systems for resource planning, such as MRP, MRPII and ERP systems
- Design and development systems eg CAD/CAM

An **intranet** is a set of networked and/or internet-linked computers. This private network is usually only accessible to registered users, within the same organisation or work group. Access is restricted by passwords and user group accounts, for example.

An **extranet** is an intranet that has been extended to give selected external partners (such as suppliers) authorised access to particular areas or levels of the organisation's website or information network, for exchanging data and applications, and sharing information.

Procurement-focused extranets usually provide suppliers with:

- Real-time access to inventory and demand information
- Authorised report information eg their vendor rating analysis.

E-sourcing tools:

- E-catalogues
- Supplier portals and market exchanges
- Online supplier evaluation data
- E-auctions
- E-tendering

An online catalogue is the electronic equivalent of a supplier's printed catalogue, providing product specifications and price information. However, an interactive e-catalogue also includes:

- Integrated stock database interrogation
- Integrated ordering and payment (e-commerce) facilities.

To be effective online catalogues should provide the following facilities.

- User-friendly navigation
- Comprehensive, focused information content
- E-commerce facilities

Benefits of e-auctions:

- Efficient administration and reduction in acquisition lead time
- Savings for buyers
- Improved value for buyers
- Access for buyers to a wider range of potential suppliers
- Less time 'wasted' on interpersonal interaction
- Opportunities for suppliers to enter previously closed markets
- Opportunities for suppliers to gather competitor and market pricing data

Criticisms of e-auctions:

- Online auctions are based on a zero-sum, adversarial or 'win-lose' approach.
- Suppliers are vulnerable to coercion.
- There may be long-term adverse effects on the economic performance of the supplier.
- There may be long-term adverse effects on the economic performance of the buyer.
- Promised savings may not materialise.
- Suppliers get the message that price is the most important factor.

P2P systems

Once an e-requisition has been confirmed, the buyer may specify the selected supplier (where relevant) and the system generates documentation for procurement, accounts, acknowledgement, receiving and inspection. There should be functionality for validation of suppliers and pricing, and an automated routing system for budget and management sign-offs. Desk-top procurement systems generally also allow users to place electronic call-off orders with approved suppliers, within the framework of a supply contract already set up by the procurement function: for example, a framework agreement or a systems or call-off contract, or e-catalogue ordering (for amounts up to certain pre-approved value thresholds) from approved supplier catalogues.

Electronic contracts can be created and transmitted to suppliers (and other relevant stakeholders). This has particular value-adding benefits, in:

- Enabling the 'cutting and pasting' of standard contract terms
- Enabling strong controls over confidentiality

- Enabling strong contract variation, change and version control
- Integration with a contract management database.

All stages of the P2P cycle can effectively be computerised, with tools such as:

- Electronic data interchange
- Online track and trace
- Expediting by exception
- Receipt and inspection
- Invoice management and electronic payment
- Contract management systems
- Database information

Benefits of electronic P2P systems:

- Streamlining and improving the flow of work
- Improved interface between the organisation and its suppliers
- Reduced error rates, associated with data input, transfer and processing
- Procurement and finance personnel freed from purely administrative burdens
- The system provides for procedural consistency, compliance and control.

Data integration

Three levels of collaborative technology:

- Electronic communication tools:
- Electronic conferencing tools
- Collaborative management tools

Collaborative technology will usually require significant levels of training to convince users of its capability and teamworking potential – and to overcome resistance to cultural change. However, there is also a technical challenge, arising from the need to integrate buyer-side and supplier-side ICT systems. Here are some integration tools:

- Extensible mark-up language
- Application programming interfaces
- Open source software
- Cloud computing
- Integrated supply chain management software

Data integrity

'Data integrity' refers broadly to the quality and 'trustworthiness' of data: the extent to which it is accurately captured, input and transcribed; kept free from corruption, distortion, errors and inconsistencies; subject to robust editing, change and version controls (to prevent confusion arising from different versions in circulation); kept up to date (and retained, discarded or archived as appropriate); and utilised according to agreed protocols and procedures (for 'housekeeping', security, data protection, confidentiality and so on).

Data integrity has four basic dimensions.

- Completeness or adequacy for its purpose
- Timeliness, currency or up-to-dateness
- Accuracy (in the sense of correctness or freedom from error)
- Validity (in the sense of internal consistency and/or authorisation).

Relevance of information risks to procurement:

- Data security and integrity represents a key category of business risk, which must be managed to secure sustainable competitive advantage.
- Effective procurement and supply chain management depends on the gathering, use and sharing of appropriate, well-structured, relevant and reliable data and information.

Risks to data security and integrity:

- Unauthorised access
- Industrial espionage, data fraud and data theft
- Data corruption
- Input or transcription errors
- Lack of controlled data management, protocols and 'housekeeping' disciplines
- Systems failure, and associated data loss
- Lack of systems integration and compatibility
- Compliance risk in regard to law and contractual provisions
- Risks to the organisation's intellectual property
- Risks to the confidentiality of the organisation's sensitive commercial data
- Turnover of key personnel and/or the outsourcing of organisational activities

The role of information assurance (IA):

- Ensuring that all buyer-side and supplier-side information systems are subject to robust access controls
- Rules and protocols for the secure use of information systems
- Protocols for the backing-up of stored data
- Systems maintenance, contingency planning and back-up systems
- Database management
- Protocols and controls over data changes, variations, versions and updating
- Internal controls, checks and balances to prevent misuse of data and funds, and fraud
- Intellectual property protection
- Confidentiality of commercially sensitive data
- Training staff in the requirements of relevant legislation
- Documentation of best practice, supplier relationship histories, learning from contracts – and other value-adding knowledge and information

Own notes

CHAPTER 11

Relationship Assessment for Supplier Development

Joint performance appraisal systems

Joint performance appraisal (JPA) is a relational, collaborative approach to performance measurement and management, in which the buyer assesses the supplier's performance – *and* the supplier assesses the buyer's performance. The objectives of this approach are as follows.

- To recognise the impact of buyer-side processes and behaviours
- To identify problems within the buyer-supplier relationship
- To support long-term value-adding relationships
- To encourage collaboration on continuous measurable improvements

Benefits of joint performance appraisal

BENEFITS FOR THE BUYER	BENEFITS FOR THE SUPPLIER
Elimination of waste at the interface between buyer and supplier	Improved financial stability and ability to plan resources over longer period
Improved quality and delivery	Better payment arrangements
Shorter lead times	Improved process capability
Enables unnecessary cost to be 'designed out' of products	Opportunities to improve management capability
Improves security of supply	Improved knowledge of buyer's situation
Increases purchasing's contribution to profit	

Benefits of 360 degree feedback:

- Provide the appraised party with an opportunity to learn how multiple stakeholders and contact touch points perceive them, leading to increased self-awareness
- Encourage self-development of both buyer and supplier
- Support a more open relationship culture
- Increase the communication interface between supply chain organisations
- Provide a powerful catalyst for continuous improvement and innovative supply network thinking

Qualities that suppliers look for in a buyer:

- Fairness, transparency and efficiency of quotation and tender processes
- Efficient and fair negotiation of contract terms
- Quality of information and communication
- Prompt and fair payment of invoices
- Accessibility of the buyer in the event of queries or problems
- Constructive handling of conflicts or disputes
- Collaboration on reverse logistics
- Ethical conduct
- Fair sharing of the risks and rewards of supply, innovation and so on

In addition, a supplier may look for 'added value' factors.

- Willingness to work with the supplier to create and share value gains
- Willingness to consult the supplier when developing specifications
- Willingness to share knowledge and expertise
- Responsiveness to supplier recommendations
- 'Intelligent customer' qualities

Relationship assessment methodologies

Key issues in assessing a supply relationship:

- Whether the relationship is being suitably managed
- Contract performance
- Operational efficiency
- The quality of rapport, trust, communication and problem-solving
- The fair sharing of the risks, costs and rewards of doing business together
- How effectively, positively and collaboratively problems and disputes are resolved
- The extent to which the supplier demonstrates willingness to go beyond contract compliance to offer added value
- The willingness and potential for the relationship to develop further

Relationship mapping is a way of analysing, classifying and prioritising relationships: that is, deciding which relationships are most valuable and profitable for the organisation, and therefore worth concentrating investment of time and money in. The best known form of relationship map in a purchasing context is **Kraljic's relationship matrix** or purchasing portfolio matrix. Note also the **supplier preferencing matrix** and the **relationship lifecycle**. Finally, note the matrix of purchaser and supplier satisfaction developed by Leenders *et al*.

Balanced scorecards

Four key perspectives for a balanced scorecard, focusing on long-term 'enablers' of corporate (and supply chain) success:

- *Financial:* financial performance and the creation of value for shareholders
- *Customers:* how effectively the organisation delivers value to the customer, and develops

mutually beneficial relationships with customers and other stakeholders

- *Internal business processes:* how effectively and efficiently value-adding processes are carried out throughout the supply chain
- *Innovation and learning:* the skills and knowledge required to develop distinctive competencies for future competitive advantage and growth.

The 'balance' of the scorecard is thus between: financial and non-financial performance measures; short-term and long-term perspectives; and internal and external focus.

Working with a balanced scorecard requires identification and description of several factors for each perspective selected.

- The organisation's long-term goals
- The critical success factors (CSFs) in achieving those goals
- The key activities which must be carried out to achieve those success factors
- The key performance indicators (KPIs) which can be used to monitor progress

A typically developed balanced scorecard for the purchasing function

SCORECARD PERSPECTIVE	FUNCTIONAL GOAL	PURCHASING MEASURES
Customer (internal perspective, eg production departments)	Increase number of orders delivered on time	% orders delivered on time vs. number of deliveries due
	Improve internal client satisfaction	Internal survey trend analysis – quarterly
	Reduce number of reported stockouts	Monthly trend of reported stockouts
	Improve internal customer communication channels	Number of purchasing-led internal meetings held per month
Financial (cost reduction and revenue generation)	Achieve increased environmentally orientated focus	Cost saving achieved per quarter via renegotiated 'green' suppliers
	Negotiate and award new collaborative contracts	Number of new contracts awarded monthly
	Increase purchasing leverage via collaborative partnerships	Cost savings achieved per quarter
	Reduce purchasing administration overheads via the increased usage of vendor-managed inventory (VMI)	Number of VMI supply partnerships created per quarter and associated overhead savings ($)
Internal processes (functional efficiency improvements)	Increase number of purchase orders placed via e-procurement	Number of e-procurement orders per quarter
	Improve departmental turn time for processing requisitions	(%) reduction of cycle times per quarter
	Increase number of e-procurement suppliers	Suppliers added per quarter
Learning and growth	Increase purchasing employee training in hours	(%) of training hours vs. total available hours
	Performance evaluations completed annually	(%) of evaluations completed
	Performance evaluations with PDP targets aligned with strategic objectives (PDP = personal development plan)	Number of quarterly aligned personal development plan targets

Own notes

Own notes